Brave One

Story by Julie Mitchell

Illustrations by Elise Hurst

Rigby PM Collection and PM Plus

Sapphire Level 30

U.S. Edition © 2006 Harcourt Achieve Inc.
10801 N. MoPac Expressway
Building #3
Austin, TX 78759
www.harcourtachieve.com

Text © 2003 Julie Mitchell
Illustrations © 2003 Cengage Learning Australia Pty Limited
Originally published in Australia by Cengage Learning Australia

8 9 10 11 12 13   1957   14 13 12 11
4500284879

Text: Julie Mitchell
Illustrations: Eiise Hurt
Printed in China by 1010 Printing International Ltd

Brave One
ISBN 978 0 75 786927 3

Contents

Chapter 1	Athumani	4
Chapter 2	A Good Heart	10
Chapter 3	Into the Water	14
Chapter 4	Leaving	20
Chapter 5	A Light on the Hills	26
Chapter 6	Rescue	29

Chapter 1
Athumani

Pili walked back toward her village from Lake Rukwa, her basket filled with wild mangoes and her mind filled with images of the lake's abundant life — glistening hippos spouting water, pink-legged spoonbills sifting through the mud flats, crocodiles gliding toward the unwary, fleets of pelicans, and everywhere, the small white butterflies. The lake was a place of wonder, and Pili had hoped it would wash away her sour mood. But as she walked on, her mood only grew darker.

For one thing, it was hot and she ached for the refreshing monsoonal rains. The dry season should have ended weeks ago, but still the rains had not come and the trees and grasses of southwestern Tanzania hung limp in the humid air.

The endless heat was a burden, but Pili was more troubled by her brother, Kiondo. Kiondo and his silly poem. *Athumani, son of Ali, bravest hunter of his tribe ...*, it began, and Pili could see Kiondo in her mind, his eyes bright and his chest puffed out as he recited the words.

5

The poem described how Athumani's people had been starving, and the young man had gone alone and hungry into the grasslands. There he had followed a herd of antelope, and when the lions took an injured animal, he had fought them off and dragged the carcass home to his village.

Pili did not doubt Athumani's bravery, but she resented the effect the poem had on Kiondo. Her brother was fourteen — barely a year older than her — and they had always been close, but now Kiondo had an attitude. Boys were tougher than girls, he said. They were stronger and braver, too. No girl would have even tried to do what bold Athumani had done.

Still angry with Kiondo, Pili descended the gentle slope that led to her village. Now she could see the sheet-metal roof of Bwana Selim's store, the straw-thatched roofs of the mud houses that lined the dusty street, and among the trees, the palm-thatched roofs of the outlying huts.

I hope Kiondo is out in the cassava field, Pili thought as she walked through the village. But when she reached the worn track that led to her home, she could see him beneath the palms, untying a bundle of roots.

He looked up and gave her a huge smile. Pili's anger fell away. Kiondo was her brother and she loved him. She would forgive him and everything would be all right again.

"What do you have in your basket, little sister?" Kiondo asked as she approached him.

"Mangoes," she replied, smiling at him.

"You must have worked hard," Kiondo said. "Did you have to wrestle them off the branches?"

"No," Pili said, her anger rising again. She pointed at the cassava roots. "And I suppose you had to wrestle those out of the ground?"

"I had to dig for them," her brother stated. "The ground was dry and hard and the sun was beating down on me, but I dug up nine shrubs. Then I cut their roots away and hauled them here. It's a good thing I'm strong," he declared, stacking the roots near their hut.

Pili put her basket down. Then, determined to show Kiondo her own strength, she gathered an armful of cassava roots. But as she began stacking them, a scorpion crawled up her arm.

She screamed, and Kiondo brushed the creature away.

"Thank you," she said.

"That's all right," Kiondo said. "It's natural for girls to be afraid of things."

Frowning, Pili picked up her basket and went inside. She didn't speak to Kiondo again that evening, and went to bed early.

For a long time she lay awake, brooding, but around midnight she heard the first heavy drops of rain, and the sound was so comforting that she fell asleep.

All through the night it rained, and high above the village, a river swelled. It tumbled down from the plateau into Lake Rukwa. And since Lake Rukwa had no outlet, its waters began to rise.

Chapter 2
A Good Heart

It rained heavily for several days, and Lake Rukwa filled to the brim. Far below it, unaware of the danger, Pili's family set about the task of producing tapioca from the cassava roots. Pili beat and washed the roots, then Kiondo reduced them to a pulp. Mama strained the pulp to separate the starchy parts from the root fibers, then she dried the pellets until they formed small, pearly-white balls.

It was a long process, and Kiondo soon tired of his part in it. Soon he announced he was going to learn *The Journey of Athumani* by heart. Over the next two days he memorized the poem, reciting it so often that Pili wanted to scream.

After six days of rain, the weather cleared. In the afternoon, Mama sent Kiondo to buy supplies at the village store.

"Thank goodness," Pili said when he'd gone. "I don't think I could bear to hear one more word about Athumani."

"Don't be too hard on Kiondo," Mama said. "It's his age. And he's in a bigger hurry than most boys to grow up."

"Why's that?" Pili asked.

"When your father died, Kiondo felt it was his duty to look after us. And as he gets older, he feels that responsibility more keenly."

"So Athumani's like a hero to him because he looked after his whole tribe?" asked Pili.

"Yes," Mama said, "and Kiondo's trying to show us how brave and strong he is because he wants us to know he can look after his family."

"He overdoes it sometimes."

"I know," Mama said, "but he has a good heart, and that's what matters." She took out a red kerchief and tied it over her head. "I'm going to visit Bibi Amina while it's not raining. Would you like to come with me?"

"No thanks, Mama. I think I'll go to the village and see my friend, Costansia."

When Pili left the hut, a watery sun was shining. But by the time she reached the village, it was raining heavily again.

It was only a short walk to Costansia's house, and Pili headed in that direction.

But she did not visit her friend that afternoon. Instead, she glanced up the street and saw two things happening at once. Kiondo, his arms full of groceries, was crossing a shallow stream that flowed down the street. And coming toward him with shocking speed was a frothing, tumbling, brown river.

"Kiondo!" Pili screamed.

But it was already too late.

Chapter 3
Into the Water

Kiondo heard someone shout his name. He turned and looked down the street. Pili was at the bottom of it, waving her arms frantically. He only had a moment to wonder what was wrong with her. Then the water hit him.

Suddenly he was on his back and water was rushing over him. He gasped and tried to stand, but the current swept him away.

Kiondo rolled over and over, and the stones of the street bed cut and grazed his skin. Even so, he clawed at them hoping to find one large enough to cling to. And then he did — for a few moments — but it came loose in his hand and the current propelled him on.

He caught a glimpse of someone down-stream holding a branch out over the speeding water, and again hope flared in his heart. If he could grab that branch, he would be saved.

Swiftly, the current moved him toward it; then he was reaching for it, and by a miracle, his fingers found it.

Kiondo clung to the branch, and felt himself being pulled, at last, to safety. But the water would not give him up. It pushed against his body, almost wrenching his arms from their sockets. Overhead, the branch began to bend. Then, quite suddenly, it snapped.

Kiondo fell and the water received him almost playfully, turning his body this way and that as it swept him along.

It didn't matter, though. He was past caring what the water did to him or where it took him. His body didn't seem to belong to him anymore, and when he noticed he was face down in the water, he didn't even bother to raise his head.

He slipped into a dream. And in that dream, he was free of the water. Strong arms carried him awhile, then he was lying on the ground and someone was breathing into his mouth.

Kiondo woke suddenly, coughing up frothy, brown water. "Thank goodness," he heard Pili say. "You're back."

Gasping air into his lungs, he looked at his sister. "What happened? How did I get here?"

"You nearly drowned," she told him, and he saw tears in her eyes.

"But I was dreaming ..." Kiondo said, noticing he was the focus of a small group of people. Bwana Majiji was there, and Bibi Bahati, Pili's friend Costansia, and a boy from the neighboring village, Hamisi.

"You weren't conscious when Pili pulled you from the river, Kiondo," said Bwana Majiji.

"Pili?"

"Yes. She shouted for us to help her make a chain out into the water, and when you reached us, she grabbed you."

"Bwana Majiji carried you here," Bibi Bahati added, "and Pili breathed life back into you."

Kiondo looked up at his rescuers: Bwana Majiji — an old man; Bibi Bahati — a middle-aged woman whose joints hurt; Costansia and Hamisi — not yet fully grown; and Pili — his little sister. They had all put themselves at risk for him.

But Pili — without Pili he would not have
been saved at all. His first thanks must go to her.

"Pili ..." he began.

She cut him off before he could say any
more. "We have to get out of here," she said,
gazing beyond their little group. "The village is
starting to flood."

Chapter 4

Leaving

By the afternoon of the seventh day of rain, Lake Rukwa could no longer contain its waters. The water plummeted down in mighty torrents, flooding the valley below.

The floodwaters rose quickly, and when Pili saw water lapping around the houses at the bottom of the street, she immediately understood the danger.

"We have to get everyone out of the village," she told the group gathered around Kiondo, "and it's probably best if we split up."

"Hamisi and I could take one side of the street," Bwana Majiji suggested, "and Bibi Bahati and Costansia could take the other."

"Good," Pili said. "Tell everyone to go to Bwana Selim's store. And tell them to bring food, water, and blankets."

"What about me?" Kiondo asked as the others set off. "I can help."

"No," Pili said. "You've had a shock, and you're bleeding. I'll help you to the store."

When Bwana Selim saw Kiondo's wounds, he provided antiseptic and bandages; and when Pili told him about the situation in the village, he was even more generous.

"I'll supply anything you think we'll need," he said.

"Thank you," Pili said, cleaning a nasty gash on Kiondo's leg. "Hamisi, Kiondo, and I will need food, water, and blankets. Everyone else is bringing their own. Oh, we'll need umbrellas, too."

"What about some dry clothes?"

Pili smiled. "That would be wonderful."

"We'll need a few lamps," Kiondo said.

"And matches," Pili added. She looked up at Kiondo. "How do you feel?"

"A bit wobbly," he answered, "but I'll be fine."

She carefully bandaged his leg and disinfected the rest of his cuts and scrapes. Then Hamisi arrived, and the three of them changed into dry clothes.

Families from the village began arriving soon afterward, and a noisy discussion broke out.

"Where are we going?" Bibi Fatuma wanted to know.

"We'll need shelter," Bibi Makihio said. "The children will get sick if we have to stay out in the rain."

Pili could feel people starting to panic, so she stepped forward. "I know a place," she said. "Up in the hills there's a cave where Kiondo and I used to play. We could go there."

"How long would it take us?" Bwana Jonas asked.

"We'd be there by nightfall," Pili said, "and we'd be dry."

Bwana Jonas smiled. "Then that's where we'll go."

They left the store a few minutes later — a band of men, women, and children under bobbing umbrellas, following a young girl through the rain to a place of safety. Pili, leading the way, did not see the look of admiration Kiondo gave her.

Chapter 5

A Light on the Hills

From the moment Pili saw the water coming at Kiondo, instinct had helped her deal with immediate dangers. But now, as she walked steadily through the rain, she had time to think about other things.

She began to worry about Mama — had she and her friend, Bibi Amina, escaped the flood? And if they had, where were they now? Then there was Kiondo. The gash on his leg might need stitches, but how long would it be before a doctor could examine it?

Somewhere behind her, a child cried, and another complained that he was sick of walking. It was enough to turn Pili's attention back to the group. There was still a long way to go, and the children would need something to help them forget about their tired legs.

Pili opened her mouth and began to sing. Before long other voices joined hers — first, Costansia's sweet treble, then Bwana Majiji's deep base, then the high piping voices of the children. Soon, everyone was singing, and Pili felt her own heart grow lighter.

Nearly an hour later, the travelers reached the cave.

Pili sat by Kiondo. "How's your leg?" she asked.

"Not bad," he said, but his voice sounded strained, and she could see that he was shivering.

"You need to get warm," she said, then she left him and headed for the back of the cave.

Branches that the two of them had dragged inside to play with a year ago were still there, and now she pulled them toward the mouth of the cave. Hamisi saw what she was doing and came to help, and soon they had a fire blazing.

As night fell, people ate by its light. And later, they camped beyond it and prepared to sleep, knowing it would guard them against wild animals.

Pili would not let herself sleep, though. She watched over Kiondo, leaving him only to add fuel to the fire. She noticed that the rain had stopped. And later, she saw a light moving over the hills.

Chapter 6

Rescue

Then she heard it — the unmistakable sound of a helicopter. Quickly she built up the fire hoping the pilot would see her signal. Then she woke everyone.

Moments later light flooded the cave and a man wearing a rescue uniform appeared at its entrance. "We've come to take you to the emergency shelter at Mbeya," he said. "Is everyone all right?"

"My brother needs a doctor," Pili said. "He has a bad gash on his leg."

"We'll take him in the first group, then. He'll get medical treatment as soon as we arrive."

Satisfied that Kiondo would be well cared for, Pili stayed until most of the villagers had been flown out. Then she joined the last group aboard the helicopter.

Dawn broke as she flew toward Mbeya, but there were no villages to see below. Instead, there was a flat expanse of water, as if the sea had grown tired of staying where it was and had moved overnight.

When Pili reached the shelter, Mama was waiting for her; she and Bibi Amina had been rescued from a hilltop some hours earlier.

"How's Kiondo?" Pili wanted to know. "Has he seen a doctor?"

"Yes," Mama said, "his leg's been stitched and he can't wait to show it off."

Pili laughed. "It sounds as if he's back to normal."

"Come and see for yourself," Mama said. She led Pili to a makeshift bed where Kiondo sat, busily writing.

"You look much better," Pili told Kiondo. She glanced at his notepad. "What are you writing?"

"A poem," he said. "It's about someone I admire — someone who's strong and clever and selfless."

Pili groaned. "Not another poem about Athumani."

"No, little sister," Kiondo said, passing the notepad to her.

Pili read the first two lines of the poem, then her eyes suddenly blurred and she held the notepad out toward Kiondo.

He gently took it from her. Then, putting his arm around her, he began to read aloud:

Pili, daughter of Lake Rukwa,

Bravest girl I've ever known . . .